EXPANDING
MEDIUMSHIP

Exploring the Ways the Universe is Communicating

Phyllis Okon

Copyright © 2023 by Phyllis Okon

All rights reserved.

Paperback. ISBN: 978-1-950080-12-0

No part of this publication may be reproduced, stored in a retrieval system, or transmitted in any form or by any means, electronic, mechanical, photocopying, recording, scanning, or otherwise, without the prior written permission of the author.

Limit of Liability/Disclaimer of Warranty: This publication is designed to provide accurate and authoritative information in regard to the subject matter covered. It is sold with the understanding that neither the author nor the publisher is engaged in rendering legal, investment, accounting or other professional services. While the publisher and author have used their best efforts in preparing this book, they make no representations or warranties with respect to the accuracy or completeness of the contents of this book and specifically disclaim any implied warranties of merchantability or fitness for a particular purpose. No warranty may be created or extended by sales representatives or written sales materials. The advice and strategies contained herein may not be suitable for your situation. You should consult with a professional when appropriate. Neither the publisher nor the author shall be liable for any loss of profit or any other commercial damages, including but not limited to special, incidental, consequential, personal, or other damages.

For David

I asked for help. You heard my call.

CONTENTS

Chapter 1 | 1
Chapter 2 | 17
Chapter 3 | 33
Chapter 4 | 39
Chapter 5 | 47
About the Author | 51

CHAPTER 1

WHEN YOU WATCH many mediums on television or at a venue, you'll notice that sometimes they scribble absent-mindedly on a pad as they connect with the spirit world.

Some say that this activity occupies their logical mind allowing their subconscious to read thoughts that are being blocked out. In other words, the repetitive motion distracts the cognitive part of the brain from the more dormant side so it can dominate.

It can be doodles or mindless scribbles, but sometimes those notes can translate into information directly from spirit, the angels, or your spirit guide.

You may not even realize it, but you might be getting messages from the universe while you scribble in the margins of your notebooks.

Mediums, seers, and psychics have all sorts of tools at their disposal that have been available for eons. They have used automatic writing, Nordic runes, tarot cards, crystals, dowsing rods, pendulums, tea leaves, and even bones or animal entrails.

The image of someone's great-aunt Thelma turning over coffee grinds or tea leaves and telling a rapt audience Mr. Right is around the corner is a comic image we all can relate to. The question begs, does that method work? Can you find accuracy in the sludge at the bottom of your china cup? *What exactly is she seeing?*

The truth is, Great Aunt Thelma doesn't see anything in the cup; her inner eye and experience are interpreting the information. She may have a few *clairs* up her sleeve, i.e., clairvoyance, clairsentience, and clairaudience, but she will allow the *Rorschach* design of the tea leaves to take credit for her intuitive abilities.

Images we see with our inner or third eye are based on what spirit or the Universe is sending. The shape of the coffee or tea confirms what Great Aunt Thelma already knows. Whether it's theatrics or justification, she uses the tool to validate her response.

Do these tools bring the message, or are we using them intuitively? *Are they some form of magic?*

It makes us wonder what their purpose is and why practitioners use them.

All of these aides are there to help hone mediumship and psychic abilities. They are used to channel the information without impacting the quality of the reading. Simply put, they are guideposts to navigate a reading and reinforce the validity of the data.

The information is already there and has been for all time. Many of these tools are used to stimulate your mediumship muscle.

For example, clairvoyance delivers messages using images externally or internally with the mind's eye. Tarot cards may stimulate a vision or instill confidence and direction in what the medium already knows.

When famed Medium Tyler Henry does his reading, he scribbles on a pad to turn his gift on and off. He discovered it while doodling on the phone with a buddy as a teen. He claims it is not the artwork that helps him focus; it's the repetitive activity.

He cites that in many religions, repetitive activities help people focus, like the mala beads, rosary beads, or chanting.

Tyler claims that *clair* sense uses his other senses to communicate information. He gets images, audibles, feelings, smells, and tastes from the spirit on the other side. He sometimes feels what spirit feels, or he'll get a mental image that is similar to one of his memories to help decipher the information.

He says his job is translating these feelings into an explanation for the client. Tyler uses a symbolic word bank, a collection of information and images he references.

For example, if he is sitting with someone whose father is John, he'll see another client whose father has the same name. That will direct him to apply the information in the current reading.

His doodling facilitates the messages, but is not providing the information.

The same could be said with crystals. Signs or messages from combinations of specific stones can be interpreted by using claircognizance or *clear* knowledge. Rose quartz may suggest a new romance is happening or soothe a relationship in trouble. Citrine indicates financial security and signifies optimism for a new job, career choice, or business.

Crystals

One of the most popular tools mediums use today and throughout history is crystals. They surround themselves, wear them, store them in pockets in their clothes, or scatter them all over their homes and offices. Crystals are minerals that vibrate at the same frequency as the human body. It is said  that we exchange energy with crystals when we work with them. People attribute many types of powers to crystals, including healing the body, mind, and soul or even bringing great success and wealth. Practitioners believe that setting an intention of crystal healing can help focus, emotional issues, and balance the nervous system and immunity.

Crystals have been treasured by humankind for as long as we've existed. Used as talismans or amulets, they've been excavated from graves dating back to the Upper Paleolithic period (60,000 years ago).

The word crystal comes from the Greek word for ice. Greeks thought that clear quartz was water that was so frozen it became permanently solid.

Amethyst, a purple stone, was worn by Greeks to prevent drunkenness and hangovers.

Hematite was rubbed all over the bodies of soldiers with the belief they'd be invulnerable in battle.

Ancient Egyptians used emerald, clear quartz, carnelian, lapis lazuli, and turquoise in their jewelry to promote good health and protection against danger. Topaz and Peridot were enlisted to fight nightmares and evil spirits.

Malachite and other green stones were used to represent the heart of a deceased person in burials in both Egypt and Ancient Mexico.

In Ancient China, Jade was the stone of choice used for everything from healing and protection to gaining wealth. Chinese emperors were even buried in jade armor. It was considered a stone for good kidney health in China and South America. The Maoris of New Zealand pass down their jade pendants from generation to generation for protection and luck.

Throughout the Middle Ages and Renaissance in Europe, crushed crystals were used alongside herbal remedies to treat sicknesses. They believe they promoted the flow of good energy.

One of Henry VIII's advisors stole one of his crystals to give to his enemy. It was rumored the stone made the wearer invincible.

However much power and magic people attributed to their crystals, they believed that they could also contain negative energy. Rigorous rituals of cleansing stones were created to protect the wearer from a sinner's contamination.

Today, practitioners regularly cleanse and reprogram their crystals before using in healing.

Aside from ornamentation and decoration, crystals are used for many essential household objects. They power lasers, watches, televisions, and other vital equipment.

In the twentieth century, and with the emergence of the New Age culture, crystals re-emerged as a healing tool.

It has become more mainstream as an accepted alternative therapy, with many colleges offering it as a qualified subject.

So, check out your local crystal shop and see what crystals *speak* to you.

There are thousands of crystals. Here are a few popular ones.

Popular Crystals

Adventurine: is said to calm negative emotions.

Agate: keep things balanced.

Amethyst: is used for healing and cleansing.

Black Obsidian: removes negative energy and toxins.

Bloodstone: is said to improve circulation.

Carnelian: stimulates creativity

Clear quartz: a clear crystal is considered a healing crystal and is believed to support the entire energy or chakra system by balancing your aura.

Citrine: sparks enthusiasm and creativity.

Garnet: is a stone of health and devotion.

Howlite: helps with meditation.

Jade: a well-known stone for prosperity and luck.

Jasper: is a nurturing stone said to provide comfort during times of stress and anxiety.

Labradorite: shatters illusions, reveals the truth, and helps with suppressed memories.

Lapiz Azuli: opens the third eye and helps interprets dreams.

Lava stones: is good for grounding and stability.

Lemon Quartz: called 'the merchant's stone,' produces income.

Malachite: helps with changing situations.

Morganite: called 'Divine love' builds self-assurance.

Moonstone: is good for digestion.

Onyx: balances male and female energies.

Rose Quartz: is used to feel unconditional love and peace.

Sapphire: considered a stone of prosperity.

Smokey Quartz: absorbs negative energies and is a protective stone.

Sodalite: brings order and peace to the mind and rational thought.

Tiger's eye: lessens fear.

Turquoise: attracts good luck.

White Jade: is a healing stone.

Palm Readers

Palm reading, or palmistry, has been around for a long time.

A Hindu teacher wrote a book about palmistry containing five hundred and sixty-seven stanzas thousands of years ago. The book's name was The Teachings of Valmiki Maharishi of Male Palmistry. From India, it spread to Tibet, China, the Middle East, and finally, Europe.

William de Hamon studied the palm and its many meanings in the late 19th century. He claimed that the brain created the palm lines to form specific patterns. He was known as Cheiro and is considered the father of modern palmistry.

Trained palm readers use different symbols and markings on the palm to determine past, present, and future. Other creases and wrinkles indicate information about careers, job security, finances, love, fame, and happiness.

There are twelve lines on the hand, the heart, life, and headlines being the most important.

The hand used for writing describes your personality. The right hand represents your present life, your left, the past.

Only the hand you are most active with should be the one read.

The small lines on your hands change every six months, except for the ones on the thumb. Lines or creases don't fill in until a person is fully grown at eighteen.

Palmists categorize the shape of hands into four classifications, Earth, Wind, Water, and Fire. The hand represents a person's strengths, weaknesses, abilities, and individuality. Fewer lines on a hand is a great sign and represents money and good fortune.

Palms aren't the only tools used to predict a person's future.

Ancient Chinese medicine maps moles on a face to predict a person's life path.

Crystal balls, black mirrors, and even dishes of water reveal visions buried deep in their depth that only a practitioner may see.

A medium or psychic may take a crystal ball, ask a question, spin it, or stare into it to gain insight into the sitter.

Dowsing Rods

Dowsing rods are another tool that has been used since the beginning of humanity. There are etchings of pharaohs from Ancient Egypt using dowsing rods, and a pair of ceramic rods were taken from a thousands-year-old tomb.

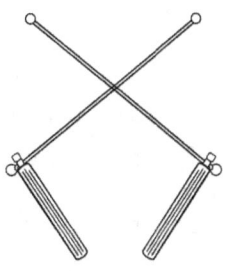

Ancient China also has two-thousand-year-old illustrations of an Emperor holding pronged rods.

Even passages in the Bible refer to divining rods to find water.

Dowsing was practiced on the ancient island of Crete and even Homer refers to it in his works.

Dowsing rods are simply two bent brass or metal rods that respond to yes and no questions, similar to a pendulum.

First, you'll need to find out which spirit is helping with the rods. The reader asks if their spirit guide or names of a specific ancestor is helping with the answers. Once the rods cross, you know who is assisting.

Holding the rods in both hands, the reader asks the rods to identify affirmative and negative.

Example Question- Grandma, will I be accepting my new job?

Dream Interpretation

Dream interpreters analyze messages received when a person relates their dreams. There are hundreds of dictionaries describing symbols and what they represent.

Dreams send us messages in metaphors. For instance, if you dream that you are too close to the end of the cliff or stairway, it may mean that you are in a risky position.

When a person dreams of mountains or hills, they represent challenges and obstacles.

A medium connects the dream with what is happening in a person's life.

Are they in a shaky relationship, or is their job in jeopardy?

The sitter knows that their gut or the universe is trying to communicate with them, and the medium verifies this information by explaining the dream.

Pendulums

Pendulums, too, have been around for thousands of years. It is said that the Oracle of Delphi used a pendulum to answer her client's questions.

Pendulums were widely used throughout history to determine the gender of a child.

Pendulums reveal the past and future by asking an affirmative or negative question. They are simply a string with a bead or crystal at the end of it.

A psychic or medium asks the *yes* or *no* question, and the pendulum moves in a certain way indicating an answer. The pendulum works by allowing the sitter to understand what their subconscious mind is not allowing them to see.

Does that mean that a person cannot read without these tools? No, but in some cases, it serves as a lodestone or confirmation.

Numerology

Some intuitives feel that they must have factual knowledge that satisfies both sides of their brain, and here's where numerology and astrology come into play.

Numerology is the science of numbers. Numerologist use numbers reflecting birthdays, ages, karmic cycle numbers, and those that match the alphabet representing their name to predict a person's future. Numerologists believe that everything in existence connects through numbers. Specific numbers hold mystical powers providing insight into understanding the meaning of life.

Numerology is said to have come from Babylonia and Egypt. People believed that numbers held power and were a gateway to the divine.

Numerology provides discernment into a person's life path, helping them make intelligent decisions based on the vibrations and formation of these numbers.

Astrology

Astrology mixes birth signs and the effects of the stars and planets to determine a person's future.

The study of the stars and planets in the sky has been around since the dawn of humanity. The Mesopotamians recorded the eclipses, stars, and planets and used their findings to study omens and predict the future.

The Babylonians divided the heavens into twelve areas and assigned a name, character, and meaning to each one. This later became known as the Zodiac. They are credited with creating the meaning and context of how horoscopes are determined today.

They claimed that the position of the stars and planets reveals a person's personality and future. Its popularity grew as the concept of astrology traveled. Numbers and calculations made it easy to cross-cultural barriers.

Trained astrologists use twelve zodiacs and assign strengths and weaknesses, desires, needs, and personality traits to form a life path of an individual.

They study the movements of the planets, Sun, and Moon from the precise moment of a person's birth, giving an idea of their flaws, attributes, weaknesses, and strengths.

These sciences have been used in various cultures, and many decisions, from marriages to when to go to war, have impacted world history.

Psychometry

Psychometry is the ability to touch an object and gain information about the person with whom it is associated. They use Clairtangency or *clear* touch.

A psychometry medium holds an object and can provide information about the person associated with it.

They can also touch a building wall or other objects and communicate to spirit.

Auras

Auras are fields of energy around a person's body. Our feelings affect them and can change color according to the emotion.

It is said that humans radiate a low level of electricity, known as an electromagnetic field. However, there are no scientific studies to prove the existence of auras.

All things have energy, and how they send out vibes affects everything around them. Vibes is an abbreviation of vibrational frequency, which is exactly what an aura is made of. Auras are present as a bubble of energy around a person.

People feel that an aura reflects a person's state of emotion. A person's aura may indicate whether they are happy or sad, angry or happy. If a person makes you uneasy or nervous, perhaps it's coming from their energy field or aura.

How can you see an aura?

Detecting an aura is as simple as softening your gaze and having a long stare. It does take practice, though.

Tarot

Finally, the beautiful and creative tarot deck. Tarot is one of the most popular and well-loved tools mediums and psychics use. Reading tarot is an intuitive art. However, how a person perceives the information is based on how they design the cards in a spread. A spread is the designated layout of the cards.

It is claimed that the tarot was manufactured with magic from an ancient Egyptian book, but the history of tarot is much less mysterious.

Tarot was created as a game of entertainment in fifteenth-century Venice. It was later turned into the mystical deck we use today in France during the 1700s. Jean-Baptiste Alliette assigned the meaning to each card and used them to speculate the future. Reading a tarot deck can be an adventure for the sitter and the reader.

Sound complicated?

It is. It takes years of study to master many of these fields.

Do you have to employ them?

No, but you should explore them and delve into their many aspects. You may find a proficiency you didn't know was there. These tools may enhance your reading style, validating the information you receive.

However, remember that the information stays the same, just the delivery method.

CHAPTER 2

Let's Unpack Tarot

TAROT IS USED in two ways. Random cards can be selected to reveal the answer to a question, or multiple cards are set out in a pattern called a spread to give insight into the past, present, and future. Each card represents a different persona or a lesson. Different styles of spreads are used for various questions. The tarot spread will guide the direction of the reading. Some assorted spreads are *Three Card, The Celtic Cross Spread, The Relationship Spread, The Career Path,* and the *Horseshoe Spread*. Each one responds to specific questions.

The reader shuffles the cards and informs the sitter to think of the question they want to be answered. The medium lays them out in various patterns representing the past, present, and future. An answer is determined by the cards showing the sitter some message or direction in their life.

There are seventy-eight cards in the tarot deck. Twenty-two are called the Major Arcana. The Major Arcana is a twenty-two-card set within the tarot. It is considered the foundation of the deck. They represent a story involving an innocent fool and his journey to spiritual enlightenment.

The remaining fifty-six are the Minor Arcana. The cards are divided into four suites, Cups, Wands, Swords, and Pentacles. The numbered cards include a Page, Knight, Queen, and King.

See a pattern here? *Clubs, Hearts, Diamonds, and Spades.*

How do you read Tarot cards?

There are four steps to reading tarot cards.

First, think about your question, then select a tarot spread with positions that relate to the question.

Next, shuffle the cards and lay them out in the selected spread.

Finally, the reader interprets the cards using their intuition.

For brevity, we will discuss just a few cards and spreads.

The Three-Card Spread

The Three-Card Spread is a quick and easy one to master. The deck is shuffled, and three cards are picked facedown. They are turned over one by one.

The first card represents the past and the events that still affect you.

The second card stands for the present and the challenges along the way.

The third card represents the direction or outcome of the sitter's situation.

The most popular spread is The Celtic Cross. It is comprised of ten cards. The following represents the meaning of each card.

1- Current situation.

2- Obstacles and challenges in the way.

3- potential opportunities.

4- the foundation of the situation.

5- the past,

6- the present,

7- the future

8- the sitter's attitude toward the situation.

9- sitter's hopes and fears

10- the potential outcome.

Reading the cards

1- The sitter provides the question. It can't be answered with a *yes* or *no*.

Sample- *What should I do about my boyfriend?*

How will I do with the new project?

2- Hold the Tarot cards and tap the deck a few times to spread your energy.

3- Think of the question.

4- Shuffle the cards as long as you like, then choose the spread you want.

5- Sometimes, cards jump out of the deck. You can either cast them aside or include them in your spread.

Card Meaning

I love it in a movie when a person pulls the death card, and the music swells with foreboding. The death card does not mean death. It indicates that something is about to change. Transition is coming.

Most of the cards in the deck do not represent what you think they do. The reader must familiarize themself with not only the meaning of the cards but what is actually in the representation.

The Fool Card.

The Fool card is an illustration of a young person walking happily in the world. He is taking the first steps on his trip and is thrilled to be in the world. He carries nothing except a small sack, and we know he cares nothing about the possible dangers on his journey.

He might fall off a cliff if he takes just one step more. He seems unconcerned. We are wondering if he is oblivious to everything around him. His trip is in danger of ending if he does not become more aware of his surroundings.

THE FOOL

The card tells a story, but what does it all mean?

The Fool card is number 0 in the deck. This number indicates untapped potential. Our fool is a blank slate; he is a symbol of innocence. Life's hardships have not yet shaped him.

When we pull the Fool card, it represents the beginning of a new journey. This undertaking is filled with joy and hope. The Fool is not attached to constraints to get in the way.

Anything can happen, and opportunities are all around him. The world is his oyster, his for the taking. He is stepping forward filled with optimism.

The Fool presents as naive courage; his perception is that every day is a chance for new opportunities. He anticipated them with curiosity, joy, and awe.

What does this mean in a reading?

The Fool card represents risk-taking or new adventures on the sitter's part. Be willing to take chances on relationships or business opportunities. Move forward, boldly and unafraid, with the confidence that it will turn out fine. Have faith that everything will work out, even if you stumble.

While the Fool inspires bravery and courage, this card presents that each day is an opportunity to delve into new parts of your life, be it business, jobs, relationships, or even renewing old projects with excitement.

Either way, it encourages the sitter to meet it with optimism and happiness.

The Hermit Card

The face of the Hermit card shows a hooded figure standing at the top of a mountain, holding a lantern in one hand and a staff in the other. The mountain represents success or accomplishment.

The Hermit Card indicates that the sitter has earned enough knowledge and is ready to share it with others.

THE HERMIT

Inside the lantern he is holding is a tiny star called the Seal of Soloman. This symbolizes great wisdom. The staff held in the other hand, represents power and authority.

Altogether a powerful card.

What does it mean?

The Hermit is a lonely wanderer searching for something that can only be found on a solitary journey. He is listening for his inner voice, the knowledge of the world that can only be found within.

He must separate himself from the tumult and noise of people to hear the messages by walking alone at night with only the light of the northern star as his illumination. His destination can only be self-awareness.

This card indicates that the sitter needs to reflect, disconnect from the noise of our busy world, and reawaken with their authentic self. If the question is about a relationship, the sitter may need some time alone to gain insight about themselves before accepting a romantic relationship with another person.

They might be lonely, but it's a time to consider what has gone wrong before and prevent it from happening again. It's time to think about what they want from a relationship and search for a way to build a strong foundation in the next relationship.

Career-wise, the Hermit card tells you it is time to think about what you want. A job might not work out right now, and your sitter may not feel satisfied with where things are going. This card encourages the sitter to dig deep and reflect on what makes us happy. Sometimes work is not about money, success, or financial security. Sometimes it's about being happy. This card indicates it may be a time to reevaluate your choices and understand what will bring true happiness.

Five of Pentacles

Like the fives in the other suites, the Five of Pentacles symbolizes adversity.

FIVE OF PENTACLES

The illustration on the card shows a person walking in the snow. She is cold, hunched over, and looking desperate. There is a building behind her with a huge window featuring the five pentacles, giving the impression of a church.

Some may consider this card challenging, but it's all about the card's placement in the spread.

What does it mean?

When someone gets the five of Pentacles, it suggests a period of hardship and instability. This card represents loss, loneliness, illness, and poverty. They may be heading for a time that could be financially difficult. Changes are coming.

This card tells the sitter to sort out their finances and not take on new debt. It could even represent someone feeling they were left out in the cold.

If the question is about romance, it may mean relationships are complex; communication is not working, creating a strain.

Job or career could be shaky. It might be time to consider a change.

If it is based on a windfall or inheritance, it might be time to move on and realize it must come from somewhere else.

Two of Swords

The Two of Swords symbolizes confusion when forced to make difficult choices.

On this particular card, a seated blindfolded woman holds a sword in each of her hands. In the background, she has a wall of water or an ocean that is obstructing her from moving on.

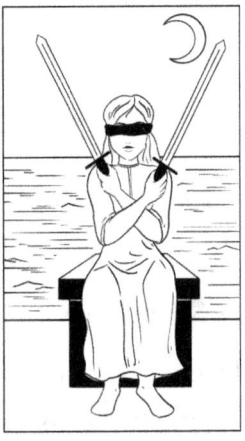

TWO OF SWORDS

The woman in the card being blindfolded represents a situation that stops her from seeing both the problem and the solution.

The swords she holds in each of her hands show that the two choices lead in different directions and are mutually exclusive.

It also depicts a stalemate, which means that the problem should be addressed with logical thinking.

The Moon on the right side of the card signifies the role of illusions or deception as the woman has difficulty making a choice.

What does it mean?

The Two of Swords indicates we are encountering a stalemate. Two equal but opposing forces are locked in battle with no end.

The sitter is caught in the middle. Without something or someone to intervene, this could continue indefinitely. A choice must be made.

One can side with one part of the situation or the other. There can be no more progress unless they can move past this stalemate.

The Two of Swords is often related to balance and partnership.

It represents the need to keep relationships balanced.

Regardless if it is in business, friendship, or romantic relationships, There may be a struggle to maintain the current situation and may find themselves caught in the middle.

The Two of Sword's meaning may depict a warning to have caution.

Like the woman in the card, the sitter may choose to keep the blindfold on, hoping the problem will disappear.

A single person might find it hard to move ahead or they are stuck between two choices.

Six of Cups

The Six of Cups symbolize the joy of nostalgia, the comfort of home, and childlike innocence.

In the card itself, there are six cups filled with white flowers. Two children are depicted in the front, and one passes a cup to the other.

This boy is handing flowers to the girl showing the passing of traditions

SIX OF CUPS

and happy times. There is a feeling of peace and security in the illustration.

The Six of Cups represents generosity, happiness, and childhood innocence.

It can mean the desire to return to a happier time, whether childhood, teenager, or young adult.

These memories may be things from the past, which reflect that part of ourselves that might have disappeared.

The Six of Cups appearing in a reading indicates that while we may look upon the past with happiness, we must avoid getting stuck there.

What does it mean?

The Six of Cups can also mean the sitter's desire to return to a familiar place. It could be a hometown, an old friend's home, a school, or any place with much meaning.

If it appears after the Five of Cups, this card can mean a loss following a journey home.

Look to the past to find the answer to the sitter's current crisis or problem. This card says the sitter is seeking the comfort and warmth of people who unconditionally love them to face the challenges in front of them.

Romantically, the Six of Cups means there might be a renewal of the past and the good feelings that come with it.

Happy memories of a partner or an ex may be coming into play.

The Six of Cups means that time heals all wounds, and comfort is essential.

Careerwise, it's a good time to look backward on the journey to this place.

Past work can provide great lessons for building a future.

It might also mean a return to an older career or job.

Ten of Wands

A man approaching a nearby town is shown carrying a heavy load of wood, represented by ten bundled wands.

This image on the ten of wands indicates a person who has already struggled in life and has succeeded and is now carrying the harvests to his final destination.

He is not near the goal, but he has finished the most challenging part of life's struggle and needs a place to relax and enjoy his success.

TEN OF WANDS

This card shows the struggle is completed.

After spending too many resources and energy looking for elusive success, obstacles have been overcome.

Efforts will be rewarded. Days of poverty are over.

Although it sounds great, the card displays a lot of responsibilities.

The sitter must be aware that they hold the most responsibility and must prioritize problems and keep everything balanced.

What does it mean?

This card expresses how people try to burden themselves with responsibilities after success.

It is like graduating from college, getting a job, and starting to make it in the real world.

The challenges keep coming. Things like looking after parents and starting a family become a burden because, at some point, more is needed to accomplish all these responsibilities.

The general lesson of the card is that people should be moderate and understand that they cannot fix everything.

Some things must be let go, given to others, and the responsibilities shared.

Love may feel like a heavy burden with the 10 of Wands tarot.

Other aspects of life, like work or finances, may make it difficult for romance.

Sometimes, the stress gets in the way.

Everyone needs to focus on themselves before they can focus on finding a partner.

The ten of wands is a card of burden.

This principle can apply easily to work life. The ten suggests a feeling of being overloaded.

It might show too many projects to handle.

It's time to share the load with others.

Collaboration and delegation are the most excellent aids at this time. Speak up about the unfair distribution of work.

Wands- Spirit, passion, energy

Cups- Emotions

Swords- Thoughts, ideas, discussions, analytical thinking.

Pentacles/Coins- Finance, jobs, material possessions.

Aces- New ideas, shifting viewpoints

2- Choices, decisions, crossroads.

3- Creativity, Out of box thinking.

4- Positive/negative card. The table has four legs, stable, safe, calm/ boring, and stuck.

5- Change.

6- Focus, perseverance, overcoming obstacles, moving in the right direction.

7- Gaining confidence for the future. Using existing experience.

8- Stuck, many obstacles, barriers won't stop.

9- Ticking off milestones, Progression,, Motivated clarity, Moving forward.

10- Completion, Rewards, achievements.

Page- New path, Putting into action, discovery.

Knight- Charging forward, take action, make it happen.

Queen- Patience, thoughtful, pausing, clearly sees the situation.

King- Possessor of knowledge, wise, good advice, someone you can trust.

0- The Fool- New chapter, change, new journey, relationships, dreamer, naive.

1- The Magician- Mastery expertise, Can be a person in life- entering training.

2- The High Priestess- Mystery, intuition, subconscious, hidden knowledge, Something going on- step back and dig around. This card comes up when someone is blocking something.

3- The Empress- Feminine energy, nurture, growth, creativity, girl power.

4- The Emperor- Male energy, strong, forceful, the builder, leader, One track mind.

5- The Hierophant- Guidance, spiritual self-help, inner wisdom, seeking deeper knowledge.

6- Lovers- Relationships- can be friends, family, or clients. Commitment, love, partnership, duality.

7- The Chariot- Progression, highly developed moving forward, making headway.

8- Strength- Willpower, inner strength, drive/ambition, focus.

9- The Hermit- Time to think, reclusive, withdraw from the situation, lonely.

10- Wheel of Fortune- Fate, fortune, out of control, not negative or positive, Control evolves by itself, be ready for new opportunities.

11- Justice- Sings of relief, good news, card of truth, the discovery of the truth, found the correct path.

12- The Hanged Man- Inspired thinking, card of delay, stuck. Not moving forward, frustrated.

13- Death- Transformation, change, the end of something, the beginning of something new.

14- Temperance- Caution, balance, don't rush.

15- Devil- Distraction, procrastination, self-doubt, something will pull away, negative barriers.

16- The Tower- Card of disruption, rebuild, rebirth, break ups, divorce.

17- The Star- Direction, long-term plans or career change, Goals, and commitment.

18- The Moon- Mysterious, unknown, hidden.

19- The Sun- Nurture, planted seeds will grow, and health will improve.

20- Judgements- Awakening, new awareness, seeing something differently.

21- The World- Harmony, balance, finding balance, peace, and understanding.

CHAPTER 3

Symbols- what do they mean?

EVERYONE RECEIVES INTUITIVE messages, but they rarely take the time to identify the vast amount of information downloading into their heads. Have you ever had a *lightbulb* moment where you suddenly realized the answer to a question puzzling you? *Where did that information come from?*

We are receiving intuitive thoughts, ideas, images, sounds, and feelings all the time. These pieces of information are called psychic symbols.

People receive these messages in assorted ways, seeing, hearing, knowing, feeling, even smelling, and tasting. These are called the *clairs,* clairvoyance, clairaudient, claircognzant, clairseintience, and clairgustiance. Once you begin to see the pattern, you won't unsee them.

Most people wonder what each medium or psychic sees during a reading. Many think their loved one is beside them, relating life details. They need help understanding that each lightworker understands these messages differently.

Mediums and psychics work with people from all over the globe. What is spicy for one culture may be tame in another. It's all relative to the person receiving the information. It's all about perspective.

The same could be said for all aspects of life on our planet. If a medium is bombarded with messages in another language or culture or customs they don't understand, chances are things will get lost in translation. Our job as mediums and psychics is to learn to interpret the many signs and symbols spirit is sending specifically to us so that we can fully understand the message.

Being a medium doesn't mean everything is spelled out for us. Spirit doesn't send detailed messages with names and information on a ready-to-use form. They send cryptic images, symbols, sounds, smells, feelings, and tastes, teasing us with hints until the sitter has that moment when they realize they are indeed communicating with their deceased loved one.

Spirit communicates in a different way than we are used to receiving information. They send messages using every means available and are relatable to the lightworker. These tools depend on the person receiving the data and their frame of reference.

Spirit is smart and creates a message form tailored to the lightworker. Using the psychic or mediums store of memories, they enlist them in a type of game of charades.

Receiving and reading these signs or messages is a fine line that shouldn't be crossed. A medium or psychic should not impose their understanding of what a symbol means. The interpretation alone belongs to the sitter. In other words, just the facts. A medium's job is to report only what they see, hear, or feel, not embellish it with their perspective.

As the receiver, we report exactly what we see, and spirit must use the vast store of our past experiences and memories to communicate.

Learning what all these messages mean should connect the dots for both the medium and the sitter. Indeed, if the sitter doesn't get the message immediately, they will after they think about it a bit.

How to create a store of symbols

You can begin by creating a *pictionary* or *encyclopedia* of symbols you receive in your messages.

Just what is a psychic or mediumship symbol?

Symbols and images are sent to us from spirit guides, deceased relatives, and angels. They are notorious for not giving up, and if we don't get it the first time, they will try another, and another, using different frequencies until they've reached us.

Start noticing what gets your attention and then think about what it means. Do high rubber boots and suspenders mean a firefighter? Or do you hear a siren or see red? An apple might mean teacher; for someone else, it symbolizes wisdom.

If dealing with clairvoyance or images, they might send images like a birthday cake or balloons to indicate a birthday. What would inspire you to think of birthdays; flowers, cake, or a present? What images spell out certain holidays; flags for Memorial Day, champagne for the New Year, Christmas tree for Christmas?

How do we tell between our imagination and a symbol?

Messages from spirit are faster than a blink of an eye. You'll need to quickly grab the image or sound and share it with the sitter. If it lasts longer than a minute, that is your imagination.

It's important to give as much information as you can. Include as many details as you remember, such as colors, hats, objects, and clothes, but be careful, don't build a fictional story around what you see.

Some symbols are there to give direction to the sitter. A fork in the road may mean a decision must be made about career, romance, or even moving. Dragonflies in some cultures mean financial wealth; in others, intuition. Be mindful of whom you are reading for and report exactly what you see.

A choppy ocean may mean a difficult path ahead. Conversely, calm waters may mean smooth sailing ahead.

What's the difference between a sign and a symbol?

Anyone can see a sign. Signs reassure us that we are not isolated and that spirit is nearby. They know we are missing them or in need of guidance or reassurance. Spirit may send a sign to let relatives know they understand what is happening in their life. It may arrive in the form of a license plate with a collection of numbers that signify a particular date. Sometimes it's a song or an object like a feather. Rainbows, birds, insects, animals, and fictional things like unicorns and fairies can be signs. **You don't need to be clairvoyant to see a sign.** They are there to aid us in life-changing decisions or, sometimes, just to let us know we are not alone.

Castle-Building

Castle building is used when inexperienced mediums or psychics feel they must use up vacant time by creating a fairy tale from the reading. As said earlier, images, sounds, and other symbols are quick, over in the blink of an eye. When a medium describes a whole story as if it is currently going on, it is their imagination.

Example- I see an old lady sitting hunched over a sewing machine. The light bulb is swinging directly over her head. She is squinting, and there is sweat on her forehead.

A medium or psychic might see the pedal of a *Singer* sewing machine pumping.

In a separate flash, they might see a lightbulb swing overhead.

They may feel a blast of heat.

Quick. Everything is short and fast.

Don't be afraid of silence. Pauses and reconnections happen in mediumship.

What are some default signs?

1- Coins

2- Feathers

3- Numbers

4- Electrical signals- television static, a flickering light.

5- Songs

6- Small animals- frogs, turtles, birds, dogs.

7- Tattoos

8- Hearts

9- Balloons

10- Jewelry

CHAPTER 4

Breaking down a reading

READINGS HAPPEN. THEY can occur anywhere. Some mediums and psychics have certain rituals to prepare for them; others have spirits dropping in all day. Even if spirit is on speed dial, a medium should be careful about doing an impromptu reading for two reasons.

The first problem may occur if you read someone uninterested in connecting with deceased relatives. It is rude to assume that everyone believes and is emotionally ready to hear from their loved ones. Some may find it offensive. Like any other personal concept, there is a time and place for a reading.

If spirit is tapping you on the shoulder and you need to share, read the room and see if the time is appropriate. Ask if the person is open to hearing a message from someone on the other side.

Readings can also become highly emotional. You can't be sure of how grief has affected that person. They may need time to prepare themselves or even take a breath.

More importantly, you may become unpaid entertainment at parties and gatherings. Constant demands that you tune in and give a message or show proof can drain your enjoyment. As I stated before, these things have a time and place.

Sometimes there is an air of entitlement with observers and I've heard more than once that you've been given a gift, so you should share it. I wonder if they will share their expertise to teach your children for free or clean your house for nothing. Mediumship is not a gift. **It's a skill that requires practice and work to become proficient.** Even if a person is born with these abilities, they must spend time and effort learning what each signal means.

While it is important to contribute to any community, nobody should always be expected to work for free. If you do choose to donate your time, try to do it for someone who needs the reading and is not looking to find out if their boyfriend is coming back.

Even if you have a steady-paying job and do this solely for enjoyment, there must be some exchange. Donating to charity would suffice if you don't want to be paid.

Readings can be emotionally and physically disruptive for both you and the sitter.

When clients book sessions with you, they usually come with certain expectations. It's important that you set up ground rules before you begin a reading.

The Reading

To prepare, protect yourself by grounding before reading a person.

1- Ask the sitter if they are open to receiving the information. You don't have to do this if they've come to you for a reading. This is more appropriate if you are doing an off-the-cuff reading.

2- Explain how you get information. Most people are curious about how you receive messages. I tell them that I see, hear, and feel the information. They need to know and understand that the images or feelings come in quickly, and I will only say what I see without an explanation. They will have to figure out how it fits into their life. I add that it is a lot like making a puzzle of the sky.

I do all my readings with a bottle of seltzer or water and a tissue nearby. Sometimes the reading feels like a punch in the gut. I try not to get emotional, but it is hard not to feel part of the grief. The beverage is there because when spirit has passed from the lungs, heart, or neck, I occasionally feel a choking sensation. Don't worry, spirit would never hurt anyone.

3- I further explain that if I see spirit behind them, it is an older generation; parents, grandparents, or even older. Beside them are spirits that are contemporary to them, and lastly, when in front, it is a child. It doesn't have to be their child, but one they knew. Babies that have not had the opportunity to finish pregnancy do show up.

People do attend with a specific person in mind. It's important to share that you cannot control who will come through. Also, spirit does not have to be a relative. Even though the sitter might be expecting their father and his brother, an uncle, shows up, he will be in the spot behind them.

4- It's important to identify the spirit coming through with a piece of evidence. Name, a physical identification, even a smell. I've had some dads with smelly feet. However, please don't get caught up on appearance unless it plays a significant role in identifying a person. People change on the other side. They take on the appearance that makes them happiest. But that doesn't mean that it isn't essential. Grandma may have long black hair, but the person only knew them with gray hair. I had a reading where I had to mention Grandma had the longest braid I had ever seen. The color was inconsequential; the length was permanent, identifiable, and important.

I see flashes of parts of an image, the braid, a mustache, and swollen feet. I describe only what I see and try not to embellish it.

5- You will have to ask questions to prompt the sitter. There are millions of facts, data, and memories that we are fishing from. If you spew symbols at them, they will get overwhelmed. If the image of a boat flashes in your brain, you should ask, "Why do I see a boat?"

The sitter should respond that one of their relatives had a boat. The following query should be, "Are they here or on the other side?" This will help you identify the spirit you are communicating with and open the floodgates of memories.

Never ask who they are here to communicate with.

Evidence

5- Evidence is vital in a reading, distinguishing a good medium from a mediocre one. An evidential medium provides information that was not public or was highly personal to the sitter. Some examples are names, dates, tattoos, and even the way they passed. The more specific information you provide gives your sitter confidence to know you are communicating with their relative.

Any information, even if it feels inconsequential, should be mentioned. Pay attention to all five of your senses. Are you smelling stinky feet or perfume, tasting something sweet or savory, cold or hot? Please take a look at everything around you.

I will feel my eyes drawn to a dangling earring on the sitter and feel compelled to ask, "What's the story about the earrings?"

Did you hear a song on the way to the reading? Did anything in your day stand out? Spirit is with us long before a reading giving clues and eager to help. I want to add that I don't believe in bad spirits, just negative energies, so you ground yourself before all readings.

6- If you are in a group setting, you ask the audience to raise their hand if the information matches their deceased loved one or if something resonates with them.

7- Don't allow the sitter to hijack the reading by explaining. They can give directions. *Yes, that makes sense,* or *no, I don't recognize that.*

8- If you mention a name and it is unfamiliar, I tell them to leave it for now and revisit it after the reading. Usually, they will write me afterward and say they realized what the information was after they talked to someone or thought about it. This is why it is wise that they record or take notes. I ask them to be responsible for the recording because I've had too many that didn't work.

9- Every reading should have a message, whether it's *I know you were there at the end, thank you for all you did for me,* or *I didn't feel pain,* you will understand the purpose of the reading.

10- I usually close a reading by asking spirit about their last day. They will show me something to give their loved one comfort. They passed peacefully, had no pain, and heard them say to let go.

Mediumship readings are there for comfort, closure, and relief from grief. A good medium will be able to deliver the message spirit has been trying to communicate.

Spirit never admonishes, accuses, or complains. These things don't matter on the other side. They want to relieve their relatives' burdens, so they can go on and finish their own purpose on this plane. They never tell me when someone is going to pass. The absolute worst they will provide is an image of choppy water, indicating rough seas may be ahead.

Every medium knows that the future is not written in stone. Free will can change the course of anything.

Even when circumstances are horrible, they ask as well as give forgiveness.

They won't tell where the gold is buried or tell someone to retaliate against someone who hurt them. They promote peace and do not care about material items. They are amused by all the things that distract us here.

What is the responsibility of a medium or psychic?

People are grieving, mourning the loss of a loved one. They are searching for answers, closure, and peace. It is a medium's job to deliver those types of messages. It is not our place to judge or embellish the truth. Unless you're sure of what you are seeing, hearing, or feeling, please don't say it.

Your job is to report what you see, not put your own spin on it. In other words, don't build castles in the air.

A reading with a medium can change a person's viewpoint and life. Grief is oppressive, especially when someone has lost a loved one and has not had a chance to have that final conversation, to say those special words, *I love you, I miss you,* or *I'm sorry.*

Mediumship is an opportunity to alleviate some sadness and bring peace to a broken heart. More importantly, mediumship can open a line of communication and teach the grief-stricken family to find the signs so they will know they are not alone and their loved one lives on.

CHAPTER 5

Setting up a business

LIKE ANY ENDEAVOR, you should set up a legitimate business if you are giving readings.

Here is a list of what you'll need.

Business

1- Set up a corporation.

2- Bank account in the business's name.

3- You should check how much insurance you have.

Social Media

1- Facebook

2- Instagram

3- Twitter

4- LinkedIn

5- TikTok

6- Snapchat

7- Threads

8- Medium

It's pretty daunting, but if you don't get your name out there, nobody will know about you.

There is always word of mouth, but it takes a long time to develop.

Step 1-

Open up an account on Medium. Medium is an open platform where bloggers publish their work with a huge audience to build and provide a following. I produce one article a week and hope that it stirs up enough interest for people to search for me and look into my work. https://medium.com/@caroleproman

Start building up your audience here and on Facebook. Join Facebook groups that align with your beliefs. There are dozens of pages of mediums and psychics. Check out their content, begin sharing, and post some of your own on your page. https://www.facebook.com/ladyphyllismedium/

The same goes for all the other social media. Include Youtube and think about podcasting if you are so inclined.

If you podcast, invite other mediums to interview and work on building an audience. You can do it live on Facebook and Youtube, where an open forum will make you available for questions. https://www.youtube.com/@OkonBros

The name of the game is creating content. ALL DAY LONG. People love to learn about you, mediumship, and how you do it.

Make sure you book as many different mediums as you can. It's important to see different styles and learn what works and what doesn't. You can watch them on social media, but there is nothing like the excitement of being read.

Look for psychic fairs and see if you can be included.

Hand out flyers.

Contact book clubs, mah jong, bridge clubs, country clubs, spas, reiki centers, gyms, and senior centers to see if they will sponsor a mediums night.

You can find the local crystal shops in your town and see if they will allow an evening of readings.

To be taken seriously, you must treat mediumship as a legitimate business.

If you don't show up, cancel, or have an unsatisfied reading, return the money. You might lose the job, but you'll keep the client.

Don't forget to volunteer to give free readings until you can build up a reputation where you can charge.

Good luck and Namaste!

ABOUT THE AUTHOR

Phyllis Okon is the CEO of an international ground transportation company she founded with her late husband in the 1970s.

She is the award-winning and best-selling author of over seventy books, as Carole P. Roman and Brit Lunden.

Never afraid to reinvent herself, she tackled mediumship during the pandemic. She studied with many of the top mediums in the country, including Seatbelt Psychic Thomas John, Kim Russo, and Joe Sheeil.

Phyllis has set up a practice as Lady Phyllis and is available for both in-person and Zoom sessions.

She lives near her children and grandchildren on Long Island, New York.